To Chrissy, who gave me the idea, that night we screamed together in Mackenzie's tomb.—L. S-S.

To Adrià and Jana.—E. S. G.

The Book of Frights for Spooky Nights © 2025 Quarto Publishing plc.
Text © 2025 Leisa Stewart-Sharpe. Illustrations © 2025 Eva Sánchez Gómez.

First published in 2025 by Wide Eyed Editions,
an imprint of The Quarto Group.
100 Cummings Center, Suite 265D, Beverly, MA 01915, USA.
T +1 978-282-9590 www.Quarto.com
EEA Representation, WTS Tax d.o.o., Žanova ulica 3, 4000 Kranj, Slovenia.

The right of Eva Sánchez Gómez to be identified as the illustrator and Leisa Stewart-Sharpe to be identified as the author of this work has been asserted by them in accordance with the Copyright, Designs and Patents Act, 1988 (United Kingdom).

All rights reserved.

No part of this publication may be reproduced, stored in a retrieval system, or transmitted, in any form, or by any means, electrical, mechanical, photocopying, recording, or otherwise without the prior written permission of the publisher or a license permitting restricted copying.

ISBN 978-0-7112-8767-9
eISBN 978-0-7112-8769-3

The illustrations are created in watercolour, gouache and pencil on paper.
Set in Adobe Garamond Pro and Journal

Designer: Myrto Dimitrakoulia
Commissioning Editor: Alex Hithersay
Production Controller: Dawn Cameron
Art Director: Karissa Santos
Publisher: Debbie Foy

Manufactured in Guangdong, China TT052025

9 8 7 6 5 4 3 2 1

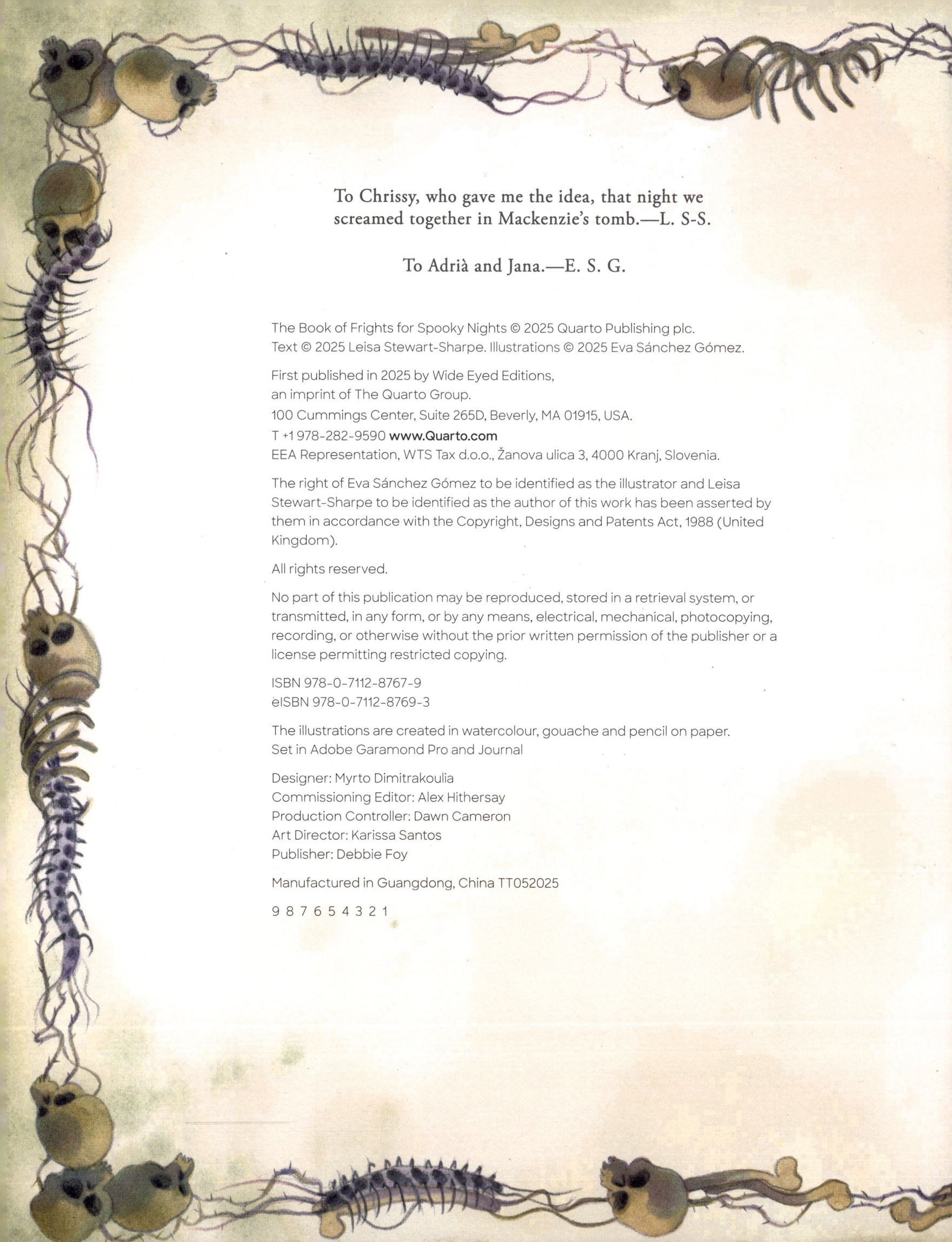

# The Book of Frights for Spooky Nights

Written by
Leisa Stewart-Sharpe

Illustrated by
Eva Sánchez Gómez

WIDE EYED EDITIONS

# IT WAS A DARK AND STORMY NIGHT...

The lightning came out of nowhere. One minute, you were hiking under blue skies and the next, you were diving for cover inside a tumbledown cabin in the woods. It's clear from the cobwebs that nobody has lived here for years. You are all alone. The only sound comes from the wild wind howling at the door, like a hungry wolf desperate to get inside.

### AND THEN IT DOES.

It squeezes under the door, skulks past your ankles, and stalks upstairs. For some reason, you follow it.

As you climb the final step your heart leaps into your throat. The attic hatch hangs open, with a light on inside. But surely that's impossible; this cabin appears to have been abandoned for years . . . And so you foolishly hoist yourself into the attic to take a closer look.

# BANG!

The hatch slams shut.

The wolfish wind makes the lightbulb swing, sending shadows dancing across the floor. Twigs scrape at the window like a witch's fingers clawing at the glass.

"There's no such thing as ghosts," you whisper.

The wind yowls, making a dust sheet billow like a ghost floating through the night. As it falls to the floor, it reveals a battered old trunk. Your trembling hands trace its rusted latch. The lock clicks, the trunk creaks, and you carefully lift the lid. It yawns open, breathing out the sour smell of mothballs and time. That's when you see them.

# BOOKS.
## OLD BOOKS.
## BOUND BOOKS.

And the one book that will forever haunt your nights.

That book is
# THE BOOK OF FRIGHTS.

The brittle binding creaks as you carefully open the book.
There, on the first mildewed page, is a warning.

My dear reader,

This monstrosity is the sum of my life's work as I have been summoned to frightful corners of this earth to investigate places haunted by their own histories. Things beyond scientific reasoning. Beyond the land of the living. Beyond your worst fears.

While I have exposed some of these places as mere hoaxes or tricks of the imagination, all too many were real. I found myself confronted by vengeful ghosts, tortured spirits, and on rare, unfortunate occasions . . . demons. And as I wrote about them, each monstrous creature became trapped inside the pages of this book.

So beware, dear reader, for this book is now cursed. Open it at your peril!

*Sigmund Bertram Campbell,*
*Ghost Hunter.*

As you read the Ghost Hunter's words you sense a cold hand closing around your neck, as though the curse of the Book of Frights is taking hold. Deep down you know you should put it down and flee this eerie attic at once, and yet the book calls to you like a whisper in the dark. What if you just took a little peek at the first page?

And with a deep breath, you begin reading the Book of Frights.

# THE TOWER OF TERROR, LONDON, UK

Torture, terror, the Tower of London. One of the most haunted sites in England.
I must know if the stories are true. After years of research, here is what I know . . .

## A frightening fortress

Fresh from the battlefield in 1066, where he had seized the English throne, the Norman invader William the Conqueror began constructing an imposing fortress—the Tower of London. With every new king, the Tower's sinister reputation grew, as gruesome history unfolded within. For as well as a royal palace, the Tower was a prison for thousands of people, and together with the nearby Tower Hill, an execution site for more than one hundred unfortunate souls.

## Don't lose your head

Prisoners would pay the executioner for a "good death" and be led to the chopping block. I am told it does not end with the sound of the axe slicing through the air, for the head has a few seconds of consciousness before the oxygen runs out. Long enough to be hoisted into the air where it might catch sight of its own body!

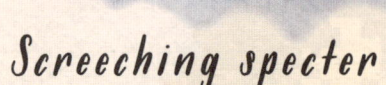

## Screeching specter

Executed for treason, the ghostly Margaret Pole, Countess of Salisbury, can be seen shrieking through Tower Green, pursued by an inexperienced axeman.

## Headless haunts

Just three years after marrying Henry VIII, in 1536 Anne Boleyn was charged with conspiring to kill him. But was her only "crime" that she hadn't produced a son? Onlookers claimed that when Anne's head hit the floor, her lips were still moving in prayer. Beware her headless spirit, drifting through the hallways.

## Wild wanderings

Animals gifted to the monarchs were kept captive in the Royal Menagerie. From a polar bear that fished in the Thames, to Old Martin the grizzly bear—enraged in life and death. Seeing his fearsome spirit is at once fatal.

Clutching the Book of Frights, I set sail for London. My first night in the Tower may well be my last.

# TRAPPED IN THE TOWER

My boat drifts under London Bridge on a rolling river of fog, as just like the prisoners of the past, I arrive at the Tower through the infamous Traitors' Gate. Those who entered this way rarely left alive . . . will I?

## Legend of the ravens

A raven lets out a gurgling croak as a Yeoman Warder, the castle's keeper, emerges from the shadows.

"Go carefully," he rasps, "the veil between the spirit world and ours is thin tonight."

It is said that in the 1600s, King Charles II was warned that if all the ravens ever left the Tower, the monarchy would fall. Since then, at least six have lived here, often fed on biscuits soaked in blood.

## To the dungeon!

I tiptoe down stone steps into the White Tower's dungeon where the air is thick with the stench of rats and something worse . . . despair. The source of it? The tower's torture devices: from the rack that stretched a person until their bones popped out of their sockets to the Little Ease, a tiny cell that trapped prisoners in an agonizing crouch.

### Whimpering wraiths

With the cries of tortured prisoners still echoing inside the dungeon, I flee upstairs, only to come face-to-face with the ghostly figures of two young boys.

"We are Edward and Richard. Please help us!" they tremble.

### An evil uncle

Hearing their names makes me suddenly remember their terrible story. When their father King Edward IV died in 1483, 12-year-old Edward was next in line to be king. But his uncle, the Duke of Gloucester, had other plans. Given custody of the boys, the Duke put them in the White Tower "for safe keeping." But when the Duke finally convinced parliament to crown him King Richard III, the boys vanished for good.

### A haunting discovery

Two centuries later, a wooden chest was found beneath this very staircase with two small skeletons inside. It's believed they were the princes, murdered by their uncle.

I write this with a heavy heart, as the spirits slowly fade into the night.

### Case closed.

# CREEPY CASTLES

## The trickster in the tower
### ZVÍKOVSKÉ PODHRADÍ, CZECHIA

I was called to investigate reports of an imp, a small demon from European folklore, making mischief for the owners of Zvikov Castle. As I entered the stairwell to the Black Tower a waft of something putrid extinguished my candle. It was blown out! Then came a sharp poke in the ribs. As I teetered on the top step, I glimpsed the trickster—horned, clawed, and beating his wings with delight. Though I suspect the rascal incapable of true evil, I advised the owners to let him have the tower to himself.

## The weeping woman
### BEIJING, CHINA

The ghost of a weeping woman in white is said to terrify night-watch guards in the imperial palace known as the Forbidden City. She faded before I could glimpse her, leaving a silk scarf floating on the breeze.

## Birth of a vampire
### HUNEDOARA, ROMANIA

I learned of tourists who spent the night in Corvin Castle and emerged terrified the next day, frightened by an angry spirit. Some say a local prince, Vlad Dracula (which in the local language means devil), was imprisoned in the castle's dungeons during the 1400s. It is said he survived by drinking the blood of rats. Centuries later, did these tall tales inspire the story of the bloodthirsty vampire Dracula, by author Bram Stoker? Although I sensed evil energy, I found no vampire.

## Wailing from the well
### HIMEJI, JAPAN

There are many versions of the story of Okiku, a maid to Aoyama Tessan, the samurai warrior lord of Himeji Castle. One of Okiku's chores was to protect ten precious plates, but one day, a plate went missing. Believing Okiku had stolen it, Tessan threw her into the castle well. When I peered into that well, I heard Okiku's ghost counting: "One, two, three, four, five, six, seven, eight, nine . . ." then a gasp, followed by a howling sob. Night after night it is the same, as Okiku relives losing the plate, and her life.

the weeping woman

# CREATURES IN THE CAVE, PENTELI, GREECE

I fear Davelis Cave like no other—a dark underworld beneath a lonely mountain. My research shows that here, just beyond Athens, thieves hid, monks lived, and perhaps ancient beasts still lurk. Explorers have lost time in the maze of tunnels underground. I hope I do not become lost for good.

## Heart of stone

In the fifth century BCE, workers were mining marble from Mount Penteli in Greece to build the Parthenon, a huge temple that forms part of the Acropolis in Athens. But as they quarried into the foot of a cliff, they discovered a crescent-shaped opening in the rock like a mouth crying out in pain. It was the entrance to a cave, where a mischievous god hid in the dark.

## A secret shrine

As the workers descended into the cave, it opened into a large hall with a pool of water at its center. Here, people came to worship the ancient pagan god, Pan. This popular god of nature and shepherds was said to have the upper body of a man and the legs, hooves, and horns of a goat. Yet for all the stories of Pan's pipe-playing and good-natured mischief, there were darker tales of his fearsome temper and terrifying shout. That feeling of panic you get when you're alone in the woods could be Pan up to no good.

## Mischief morphs

In the Middle Ages, a double-sided church was carved into the mouth of Davelis Cave—each side honoring a different Christian saint. But did the rise of Christianity, promoting the worship of one God, lead to the image of Pan changing into something evil: the devil himself?

## Strange happenings

I have read reports of hovering balls of light and water running uphill. Stranger still, stories of a choir sweetly singing in the dark. Could it be pixies, or something much worse?

My hands tremble as I zip the Book of Frights into my backpack and begin the hike to Davelis Cave.

# A JOURNEY INTO PAN'S LAIR

Mist swirls at the cavemouth like the breath of a demon as I tentatively step inside. The stalagmites and stalactites make it feel like I'm standing in the mouth of a monster, with the constant drip, drip of water, alarmingly like drool. I reluctantly begin my journey into the belly of the beast.

### Let there be light!

Rumor has it that from the 1970s, the Greek military closed the caves to the public so they could investigate paranormal phenomena, such as eerie orbs of light that hovered above the ground. Others believed they were digging tunnels to store nuclear weapons. Then one day, work was abandoned, with many tunnels left as dead ends. And I've just walked headfirst into one of them!

## Who's afraid of the dark?

I slam into the cave wall, drop my flashlight and am plunged into darkness. Luckily, I switch on my infrared camera to be my eyes in the dark. With my senses on high alert, I suddenly detect a faint sound. A scuffling followed by a sharp snort. My blood runs cold. There is something down here. And that something . . . takes up the chase.

### The chase

Stumbling through the tunnels, I can feel the hot breath of that something on the back of my neck. Glimpsing daylight up ahead, I tumble through the cave mouth into the safety of the light. But what was that thing?

### A creature in the crevice

Nervously rewinding the camera footage, I pause as a creature slowly emerges from a crack in the cave wall. It looms before me on two hairy legs, the camera light glinting off its curled horns. Its eyes gleam with wickedness as its bearded mouth curls into a smile.

IT WAS PAN.

I snap my camera closed, unwilling to watch another moment.

## Case closed.

## GO CAREFULLY IN THE COUNTRYSIDE

### Trapped in defeat
#### CULLODEN MOOR, INVERNESS, UK

Each year on April 16, the clanking of metal and the cries of wounded soldiers drift across misty Culloden Moor in the Scottish Highlands. On this day in 1746, 5,000 Jacobites took to the boggy battlefield against 9,000 English "redcoats" to restore a Scottish king to the throne. In less than an hour, 1,250 Jacobites were slain, and the moor ran with blood. I encountered the ghost of a Jacobite soldier, wounded and muttering the word "defeated" as he swept by.

### Do not look upon it!
#### SUFFOLK, UK

The beastly Black Shuck is said to roam the fens of East Anglia; a devil dog as tall as a horse with a single eye blazing. If you meet it on a lonesome night, in an empty field, or on a deserted path, do not stare into that eye, or you are as good as dead. Not even sheltering inside will save you, as in one story the Black Shuck tore down heavy church doors to reach the parishioners inside. I have heard the beastly wind howl, and I wonder . . .

## Beware the banshee
### IRELAND

Old witch, hag of the mist, woman of the fairies. Since the first accounts from the 1380s, the banshee has been feared in Irish folklore. She would appear in the Irish countryside, cloaked and red-eyed from crying, and release a shriek loud enough to shatter glass. It is believed this was a very bad omen—a signal that death was coming for you or your family. On a still, frosty night, I heard that chilling cry and looked up to see the ghostly white vision . . . of a barn owl.

## The Beast of Bodmin
### BODMIN MOOR, CORNWALL, UK

This panther-like cat is often spotted by farmers on England's Bodmin Moor and blamed for the mutilation of cattle. Official investigations say it is not so, but I saw a grainy photo—irrefutable evidence of a big cat roaming the moor. Maybe it escaped from a zoo? However it got there, I would not wish to be alone with it on the moor.

# THE PHANTOM OF THE OPERA, PARIS, FRANCE

Time does this devious thing—it distorts the truth of an event. Each tale-teller tweaks it for the sake of a good story, and over many years, fact and fiction meld to become legend. In my research, I have peeled back the layers to get to the heart of the story within.

## The two masterpieces

It begins with two masterpieces. First, the magnificent Palais Garnier opera house completed by architect Charles Garnier in 1875 for Emperor Napoleon III. Second, the 1910 novel The Phantom of the Opera by Gaston Leroux, which tells the terrifying tale of a young opera singer taught to sing by a faceless ghost—the Phantom of the Opera. Leroux claimed to have drawn inspiration from real-life events, but could a phantom really haunt the opera house?

## Unlucky 13

Palais Garnier was Paris' 13th opera house—many others were destroyed or damaged by fire, including the Salle Le Peletier in 1873. In that fire, a ballerina tragically died, and her pianist fiancé suffered severe burns to his face. Heartbroken, some say he sought refuge away from unkind eyes, retreating into the secret chambers beneath the new Palais Garnier opera house. A phantom was born!

## Avoid the 13th step

The shadow of a ballerina sweeps down the grand double staircase. It is said she lost her life when she tripped on the 13th step.

## Beware seat 13

Suspended from the gilded dome of the Palais Garnier's ceiling is a stunning bronze and crystal chandelier adorned with 340 glittering lights. Weighing as much as an elephant, it hangs by iron wires and a counterweight. But in 1896, one of the wires sparked and melted, causing the counterweight to plunge through the ceiling and into the stalls, tragically killing a woman. I heard she was sat in seat 13.

## Fact or phobia?

Many people fear the number 13, believing it cursed, in a condition known as triskaidekaphobia. It is why some skyscrapers do not have a 13th floor, and many airplanes do not have a 13th row. Could this phobia be behind the haunted happenings at the Opera House?

I slip a lucky horseshoe into my backpack and head to Paris to investigate.

# ON THE TRAIL OF THE PHANTOM

My footsteps echo in the deserted foyer as I scale the marble staircase, past statues holding torches aloft. Is it a trick of the eye, or did the light just flicker?

## Hush

At that moment, the nightwatchman hurries toward me, wringing his hands: "Please, please be quiet!" he urges. "He mustn't hear you!"

Does a phantom truly terrify everyone inside this building?

## Music of the night

Aside from the nightwatchman, I was told the building was empty tonight. So how is spine-chilling organ music now drifting down the hallway? I follow each mournful note into the auditorium, where a monstrous pipe organ mysteriously plays off-stage.

Suddenly, I'm blinded by the bright lights of the chandelier. It ominously swings from its wire, throwing light onto Box 5, where a shadowy figure looms.

### THE PHANTOM HAS COME.

## The pursuit

With a dramatic swirl of his cape, the Phantom disappears, and I'm left to chase his shadow through a maze of hallways and down into the basement. A metal grate lies open in the floor and I tentatively clamber down the ladder, one slippery rung at a time. But on the 13th rung, I slip . . . and SPLASH into the phantom's lair.

## Slithering through the cistern

I recall the building's old blueprints show a cistern located several stories below the stage. It formed when construction workers dug too deep, and groundwater began to rise. And so, the architect created this underground lake.

As I wade through each tunnel, the water ripples before me. Is it him? But with the flash of its white belly, a catfish disappears like a ghost in the night. I wonder if it's all been a trick of the imagination.

Then the organ begins to play. Someone who doesn't want to be seen, though doesn't mind being heard. I leave the Phantom in peace, and retreat into the night.

## Case closed.

# HAUNTED HOUSES

## The Banff Bride
### BANFF, ALBERTA, CANADA

High up in the Rocky Mountains in the Fairmont Banff Springs Hotel, a bride glides down a staircase lined with candles: a vision in white. But as her dress sweeps down the stairs, it ignites. She tries to extinguish it, but it is too late—she has taken her final step. I saw the bride dancing alone in the ballroom, and it was enough to make my heart break.

---

## Ship of frights
### NOTTINGHAM, NOTTINGHAMSHIRE, UK

In perhaps England's oldest inn, Ye Olde Tripp to Jerusalem, a wooden model ship is displayed above the bar. The owners tell me anyone who touches it dies; as did the last poor soul who tried to dust it. It now resides behind a glass box—I did not dare test the theory.

Ship of frights

---

## The witch's inn
### WOTTON-UNDER-EDGE, GLOUCESTERSHIRE, UK

As I first approached the Ancient Ram Inn, it looked cosy enough, as woodsmoke spiralled from the chimney, but inside was anything but. It is said there was once a woman who refused to practice Christianity—a dangerous decision in the 1500s, which was a time of widespread witch hunts across Europe. With the officials coming for her, she tried to shelter inside the inn, but was found, and as was the practice of the time, burned alive. I could smell smoke the whole night through.

---

## The Mystery House
### SAN JOSE, CALIFORNIA, U.S.

Passers-by quicken their pace; they know better than to linger outside the Winchester Mystery Mansion, a house built for ghosts. Convinced restless spirits lived in her eight-room farmhouse, Sarah Winchester transformed her mansion into a maze to confuse the spirits. Inside are miles of hallways that twist and turn, leading to thousands of doors—one dropping into the garden, another opening onto a blank wall. Staircases lead to dead ends, and a cabinet opens to reveal a secret passageway within. When I visited, I too heard the whispers in the hallway and saw something moving past the spyhole in the door.

# THE HORRIBLE REALIZATION

## I'm being followed!

I first noticed the foul stench of bear's breath a few days after leaving the Tower of London—clearly Old Martin is on the prowl. I then became chillingly aware of Pan, slinking in the shadows, as one by one, every horrid beast and disturbing specter in the Book of Frights followed me on my journey.

They are waiting ever so patiently for me to fail and for the book's curse to take hold. Only then can they cling to me forever more. Well, not if I can help it. I must be brave and finish what I have started.

# FREAKY FORESTS

## House of horrors
### EASTERN EUROPE

There is a ramshackle cottage that travels through the deep dark forests of Eastern Europe by sprouting chicken legs and walking. At first, I found the vision amusing, until I learned of what lives inside that house. It is the home of Baba Yaga, a witch who delights in stealing, cooking, and feasting on children. I passed through the fence made from skulls and bones and peered through the keyhole lined with teeth. When I saw Baba Yaga prepare to leave her house . . . I hid. For it is said she accompanies Death on his journeys to extinguish the living.

## Choose your words carefully
### NEW JERSEY, U.S.

When a distraught mother learned she was expecting her thirteenth child, it's said she cried out: "Let it be the devil!" The stories say she then went on to give birth to a creature with leathery wings, a goat's head, and hooves, and as it entered the world, it screeched and took off through the window. Even police, government officials, and experts have reported on its movements. Yet with the $10,000 reward for its capture still unclaimed, I cannot believe it to be true.

# Dancing with the devil
### NORTH CAROLINA, U.S.

The locals call it the Devil's Tramping Ground, a mysterious circle in the woods where nothing will grow. They claim to have seen red eyes glowing as the devil paces there at night. However, soil samples suggest the plants will not grow because the earth contains too much salt. I am inclined to side with science.

# The twisted forest
### CLUJ-NAPOCA, ROMANIA

There is a forest where the local people dare not tread. In Hoia Baciu, named after the shepherd who disappeared there with his flock, the trees grow in unexplainable corkscrews, spiraling clockwise toward the sun. There are reports of bright orbs of light that hover above the ground—perhaps connected to spirits. I saw it for myself, and left without delay.

# THE SHIP OF SHADOWS, LONG BEACH, CALIFORNIA, U.S.

The Queen Mary—grand ol' lady of the Atlantic. First luxury liner, then war hero, but oh, how her fortunes have since sunk. My investigations have revealed she is no longer best known for her elegance or honorable service, but as the "ship of shadows" haunted by some 150 spirits.

## The Grey Ghost

RMS Queen Mary launched from Southampton, England as a luxury liner in 1936. She ferried the rich and famous between England and the U.S. during the Golden Age of Hollywood. But in 1939, with the world at war, she was stripped of her fineries and painted in camouflage to become "the Grey Ghost." Using her stealth and speed, she outran enemy ships to carry more than 800,000 American troops to the front line. Luxury service resumed in 1947 for the next two decades, until the Queen Mary sailed into retirement, permanently docked in California as a floating hotel. Now, below deck, there are things that stir in the night.

### Don't slip

Reports say a trail of wet footprints never dries beside the first-class swimming pool—long drained of water. They belong to the ghost of little Jackie, who plays peekaboo from the upstairs balcony.

### Doorway of death

The long hallway past the engine room, known as Shaft Alley, was once the site of a gruesome accident. One night, in 1966, the watertight doors were ordered shut during a fire drill and Hatch Door 13 crushed a young engineer. He is often seen in his blue boilersuit and heard whistling as he haunts the doorway of his death. Some passengers claim to have left the area with greasy fingerprints on their faces, as the ghostly engineer reaches out to the living.

### Rooms to avoid

I will not dance with the ghostly Woman in White as she twirls across the dancefloor. And although sparkling and splendid, the Mauretania Room belongs to the Sitting Spirit who silently stares into nothingness. If approached, he dissolves like a wisp of smoke.

I prepare for a night below deck.
All aboard The Ship of Shadows.

# THE NIGHTMARE BELOW DECK

Under normal circumstances, the offer of a night's sleep on a splendidly furnished ship would be an unmissable opportunity. Unfortunately, reports say nobody sleeps in Room B340.

## Taunting tourists

I have learned that the ship's previous owner pretended Room B340 was haunted to attract tourists searching for a good fright. The disused stateroom came complete with intentionally creaky floorboards and ghostly noises piped in by the crew. But when the business failed, the door to B340 was locked and not opened again for many years. Paranormal experts claim that is when the real trouble began. They say people who visited the room, believing and then sharing made-up stories, somehow conjured the evil spirits into existence. Left alone in the room, those fake tales grew into something truly frightening. My night in the haunted stateroom has begun.

## Batten down the hatches

I waste no time latching the security chain and checking under the bed. To my relief, I am alone—very much so, as the crew has the night off. Now long past my bedtime, I climb into bed, leaving the curtains slightly ajar to fend off the dark. Before long, I drift off to sleep.

## Knock, knock.

I wake with a jolt. Someone just banged on the door, and all at once the temperature plunges, making my breath plume in the cold air. When no other sounds come, I fall back into a fitful sleep.

## Who stole the covers?

Later, I wake shivering, having somehow lost the covers, as icy claws of frost make their way up the window. But no sooner am I cocooned again, when the covers are wrenched off me. It is no accident; they were taken.

Turning on the lights, I watch in horror as the bathroom faucet twist onto full. In moments, the sink is overflowing, and water is spilling across the floor. As I fling open the door to leave, the lights to B340 go out, followed by the chilling sound of laughter.

B340 is unquestionably haunted.

## Case closed.

# ISLANDS OF DESPAIR

## Avert your eyes!
### OAHU ISLAND, HAWAII, U.S.

First, you might hear the blast of a conch shell, then the pounding of pahu drums. The Night Marchers have come: warrior spirits known across Hawaii's islands as the huaka'i pō, once tasked with protecting the ruling chiefs. I was there on the night of a new moon as the huaka'i pō drifted over the sand. I heeded the warnings to never cross their path.

## Rest in peace
### POVEGLIA ISLAND, VENICE, ITALY

When an infectious disease known as the plague returned to Venice in the 1700s, the dead and near-dead were dispatched to nearby Poveglia Island. The bodies of about 100,000 people were thrown into plague pits on the island or cremated. The soil still holds their ashes. Fishermen will not land their boats there, claiming bells still toll on the uninhabited island. I say these are wild imaginings. May their souls rest in peace.

## They came on boats
### PORT ARTHUR, TASMANIA, AUSTRALIA

Between 1788 and 1868, the British Empire imprisoned about 162,000 convicts in a penal colony in Australia. Many of the early convicts found themselves on the island of Tasmania, inside the much-feared Port Arthur Prison. Here, a thousand people died during the prison's 47-year cruel and tragic history, subjected to savage physical punishment of labor, leg irons, and lashings. Then there were those prisoners who got the silent treatment—locked alone in a dark cell for all but one hour a day, when they were allowed to venture outside in a slitted hood. The guards even learned sign language so the prisoners never heard the voice of another soul. Footsteps still echo inside these cells at night. Overwhelmed by sadness, I did not linger.

## The loathsome lighthouse
### TEVENNEC LIGHTHOUSE, BRITTANY, FRANCE

In a violent stretch of sea, west of France, is a place sailors call "hell." The ghosts of sailors who perished in those wild waters are said to haunt Tevennec Lighthouse, sending many a lighthouse keeper insane by calling for them to leave. I was relieved to find the lighthouse is now run by computers—not ghosts.

Tevennec Lighthouse

# THE DARK CITY, EDINBURGH, UK

Over the centuries, dark history has unfolded in dark corners of Edinburgh. From the poor who lived in squalor beneath the cobbled streets, to those tortured and imprisoned at the foot of a church. This investigation is a journey into a haunted past . . .

## A life on high

In the seventeenth century, the rich lived "on high" in apartments known as tenements some fifteen stories tall, while the poor scratched out a living down, down below.

## A world below

Spaced barely three feet apart, the towering tenements created a winding labyrinth of alleys and streets called closes. So named because of the gates used to close them off from the main street. They were foul-smelling places, often lit by streetlamps fuelled by fish oil. Some say they were foul looking too, as eerie lights slinked down the lanes, caused by toxic gases from a nearby polluted lake.

## Of beaks and boils

As well as living in "close" quarters with each other, residents shared their space with rats. Before long, the plague swept through the closes. In the overcrowded Mary King's Close, the plague doctor would come calling in his beaked mask, stuffed with herbs to protect him from the "evil smells" and infection. He would lance the victim's black, pus-filled boils and sear them with a red-hot poker to prevent the deadly bacteria from entering the patient's bloodstream. In doing so, he saved many lives.

## Secrets of the vaults

The plight of the poor continued in the dank vaults under the nineteen arches of South Bridge. Once used as taverns, workshops, and for storage, the arches were abandoned when they became waterlogged. Only then did they become a last refuge for the poor. Beware the ghost of the smuggler, Mr. Boots, who stomps through the vaults whispering "go away" to protect his stash. Though it is the Mackenzie Poltergeist in Greyfriars Kirkyard who I fear most—an angry ghost who refuses to rest in peace.

*A night in the world's most haunted graveyard . . . What could possibly go wrong?*

# A NIGHT BEYOND THE GRAVE

It's been drizzling for days as I step into Greyfriars Kirkyard. Taking a deep breath, I trudge toward a quiet corner of the graveyard where the gated Covenanters' Prison lies.

## The Killing Times

In the 1600s, Covenanters were Scottish people who opposed the religious restrictions being pushed onto them by the Stuart Kings, who ruled over England and Scotland. So began the "Killing Times," as for many decades fights raged between the Covenanters and supporters of the king.

Then, in 1679, King Charles II's forces defeated the Covenanters in a bloody battle. After that, the king's villainous lawyer, George Mackenzie, got to work imprisoning almost 1,200 Covenanters behind these very gates.

## Bloody Mackenzie is born

I put my hands on the iron bars to peer inside. Here, those who were not executed were left to die from exposure, torture, and starvation. Their brutal treatment earned Mackenzie the title "Bloody" Mackenzie.

## Do not disturb the dead

The drizzle turns to driving rain, and to my horror, bones begin to push up through the sodden earth, as though the dead are rising. Desperate to leave this awful place, I set off at a jog, realizing too late that the path leads me directly past Bloody Mackenzie's tomb.

## Mausoleum for a murderer

Located just meters from the site of his worst atrocities, Mackenzie's black mausoleum looms before me. The trouble with this tomb began in the late 1990s, when a man broke in and fell through the floor. With his grave disturbed, it's believed the maddened spirit of Mackenzie began attacking passers-by, leaving them scratched and bruised. The council locked the gates to stop people from getting in . . . but Mackenzie can still get out.

The lone church bell tolls as I hear knocking from inside the tomb. It grows louder and louder. Then the gates begin to violently shake.

And that's my cue . . . to go.

### Case closed.

**Holy Innocents' Cemetery**

# GHOULISH GRAVEYARDS

## Twisted tunnels
### PARIS, FRANCE

In the late 1700s there were simply too many bodies in Paris' cemeteries, causing vile odors to spread through the city. In the Holy Innocents' Cemetery, the largest in Paris at the time, millions of decomposing bodies were placed in mass graves. The overcrowding eventually put pressure on the cemetery walls, sending corpses spilling into the basements of nearby houses and taverns. Thankfully, city officials remembered an old limestone quarry wound beneath the city. Its 190 miles of tunnels would become a catacomb for around six million souls. The skeletons were quietly put in carts and removed from the cemeteries at night to line the tunnel walls with bones. I heard eerie voices coaxing me deeper into the catacombs. Had I followed, as others have before, I may not have found my way back to the light.

**Highgate Cemetery**

Boothill Cemetery

## A cemetery stake-out
### LONDON, UK

In the wooded Highgate Cemetery, tendrils of ivy wind around headstones cast in dappled light. It is a peaceful place, but it was not always so. For a time in the 1970s, rumors abounded that a tall, cloaked figure with blazing eyes haunted the cemetery, frightening walkers as he emerged from the shadows. Two local "vampire hunters" created a media frenzy when they argued a vampire was roaming the grounds, feasting on foxes, and the legend took hold. Thankfully, I saw no evidence of a vampire in my stake-outs.

## Gunslinging ghosts
### TOMBSTONE, ARIZONA, U.S.

In the Wild West of the U.S., the lawless town of Tombstone was famous for two things: silver mines and outlaws. The area's rugged mountains and deep canyons provided the perfect hiding spot for outlaws in trouble for gang fights, robbing stagecoaches, stealing cattle, and committing murder. If they expired while up to these no-good deeds, they were said to have died "with their boots on," and were buried in Boothill Cemetery. Today, the ghosts of these gunslingers haunt the cemetery trying to avenge their deaths. I hid from the ghost of outlaw cowboy Billy Clanton who died in a shootout, as he drifted through the cemetery loading his pistol.

# TROUBLESOME TOMBS, VALLEY OF THE KINGS, LUXOR, EGYPT

By day, Egypt's Valley of the Kings is filled with tourists. But as the sun sets, it is said the Curse of the Kings takes hold. Do the spirits of the pharaohs haunt the Egyptian night?

## Treasures unearthed

The Valley of the Kings is a hidden burial ground in the hills on the western bank of the Nile River. From around 1539 to 1075 BCE, ancient kings and queens known as pharaohs were laid to rest in tombs carved into the rocky valley, holding everything they would need in the Afterlife—from jewelry and furniture to pets.

## Robbers beware

Nobody was ever meant to see the pharaohs' final resting places—with inscriptions warning grave robbers to stay away. An inscription on a tomb near the Giza pyramids, near the Egyptian capital of Cairo, declares that anyone entering will face death by crocodile. Yet one tomb is associated with a curse more than any other: that of pharaoh Tutankhamun in the Valley of the Kings.

## The trouble with Tut

When Tut's tomb was opened in 1922, many believed it unleashed a curse killing those associated with the dig. The English aristocrat Lord Carnarvon, who funded the dig, died shortly after the tomb was opened, along with his pet bird and dog. The radiologist who x-rayed Tut's mummified body followed suit, as did the archaeologist who helped Carter open the tomb. An object given to one of Carnarvon's friends was even blamed for their house first burning down, then flooding.

## A creative curse

However, I believe the curse was created by journalists to sell newspapers, especially given archaeologist Howard Carter went unscathed, as did many others. Yet the guards who watch over these tombs tell me otherwise.

## Things that go bump in the night

The guards say shuffling footsteps follow them down the lonely hallways at night. Are those who were entombed here unable to make their final journey into the Afterlife, for their tombs were ransacked by grave-robbers long ago? And what of the stories of a wandering pharaoh who haunts the night?

The time has come to travel into the Valley of the Kings and discover the truth behind the curse.

# ESCAPING THE PHARAOH'S CURSE

Soft moonlight reflects off the dunes as I travel through the cool of the desert night. My every sense is heightened, as I keep a watchful eye out for the Wandering Pharaoh—Akhenaten.

## Eternal damnation

Pharaoh Akhenaten changed Egypt's religion from the worship of many gods and goddesses to the worship of the single Sun god Aten, in the fourteenth century BCE. In that one decision, he cast aside the gods and their temples, greatly angering many devoted followers. And so, legends say that upon Akhenaten's death, the priests cursed him to forever wander the deserts unable to enter the Afterlife. Travelers are warned to never approach his ghost, or they'll be cursed to join Akhenaten on his lonely travels too. Though Akhenaten's mummy was never found, some say it was hidden here in a Valley of the Kings tomb to protect it from those he had upset.

## Secrets in the sand

Thankfully, my journey is almost at an end as the Valley of the Kings stretches before me, the illuminated pillars of Hatshepsut's temple appearing to cast the hills in hallowed light. As I draw closer, I notice the tomb doorways carved into the limestone rock, leading down to magnificently decorated tombs.

## A pharaoh aflame

As I ready myself to venture underground, a high-pitched squeal cuts through the night. Two angry black stallions gallop toward me, pulling a war chariot that's been set alight. And in the heart of the fiery blaze, a man clutches the reigns. He is dressed in all the finery of an ancient king; the fire reflecting in his golden collar and headdress.

### Dive, you fool!

I stare at him, dumbfounded, when a guard thanfully breaks the spell: "Dive you fool—get out of the way!"

The horses are almost upon me as I snap to my senses and fling myself through an open doorway. The chariot and its flaming rider race on through the rock, disappearing back into the past.

I have no doubt they will return, and I will be gone when they do.

## Case closed.

# RUINOUS RUINS

## The evil amphitheater
### ROME, ITALY

Built by emperor Vespasian and completed by his successor Titus in 80 CE, the Colosseum was a huge amphitheater at the heart of ancient Rome. Here, some 50,000 spectators would cram inside to watch gladiatorial games where captive animals, such as elephants, bears, and crocodiles, were pitted against each other or enslaved fighters known as gladiators. For hundreds of years, up to half a million humans and over one million animals died in these staged battles. When I walked the underground passages, I heard low rumbling growls while the bleachers above seemed to roar with the braying masses once more.

---

## City of ghosts
### RAJASTHAN, INDIA

Built in the 1500s, Bhangarh Fort was once a beautiful palace, yet today ruins are all that remain. The story goes that an evil sorcerer was obsessed with the beautiful princess Ratnavati and tried to trick her into falling in love with him. He cast a spell on her hair oil, but suspecting something was wrong with it, the princess cast it aside. The oil splashed onto a boulder, causing it to roll onto the sorcerer. Before he was crushed, he cursed the princess and her subjects to leave their beautiful village or die. Bhangarh has been a ghost city ever since. I walked through the ruins at night with the monkeys for company and I sensed no curse, only peace.

---

## Desert djinns
### PETRA, JORDAN

In Arabic mythology, djinns (the English word is genie) are shape-shifting spirits that go unseen by humans. Many believe mischievous djinns delight in leading people astray or are the true culprits behind an unfortunate accident. Standing before the Royal Tombs in Petra are three lumps of stone called the Djinn Blocks. Some claim the blocks were carved to repel the djinns that haunt Petra at night. A rock hit me in the back of the head as I passed the blocks, but I could find no culprit.

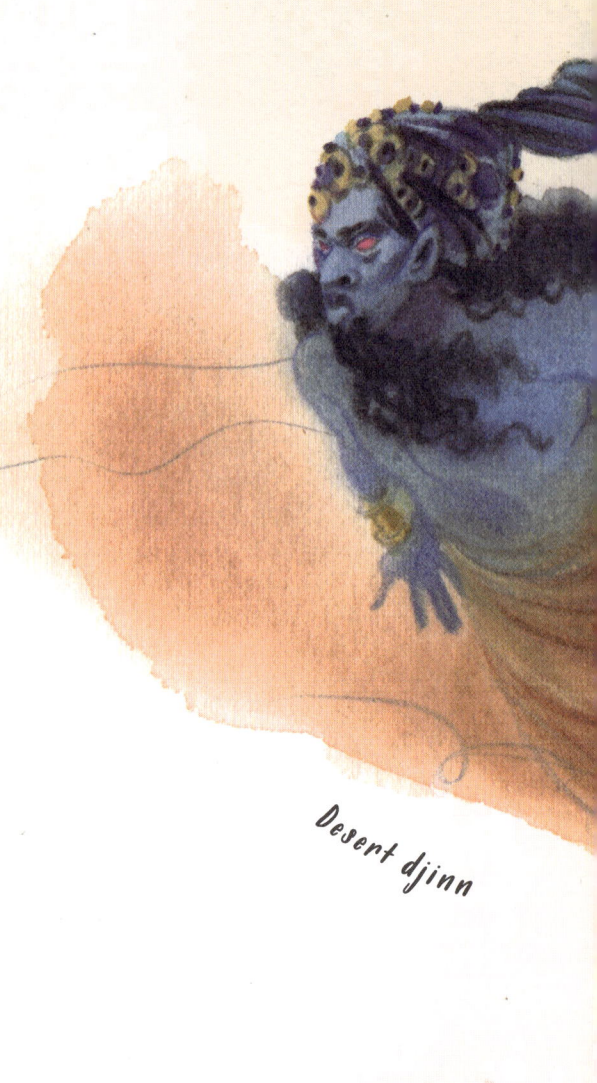

*Desert djinn*

# A TERRIFYING TOWN, SLEEPY HOLLOW, NEW YORK, U.S.

By day, the charming village of Sleepy Hollow is as pretty as a picture, with trees blazing bright in frosty fall light. But by night, fog slinks through the graveyard and coils around the headstones. The only thing that will disturb it is him. A horseman, harried and headless, who gallops through the night. The facts I have unearthed fill my heart with dread.

## A town

The tale of Sleepy Hollow begins on the banks of the Hudson River, where in the 1600s, Dutch settlers built a village known as Tarrytown, in what is today the state of New York. Later that century, Tarrytown was passed over to the British, as King James I began establishing colonies along America's east coast.

## A revolution

The local people resented paying taxes to the king without having any say in their government, so they rose up to reject British rule in a war for independence. So began the American Revolution from 1775 until Britain's defeat in 1783.

## A battle

One battle between the American rebels and British troops, supported by German "Hessian" soldiers, took place near Tarrytown around the time of Halloween in 1776. During the battle, it is said a cannonball flew across the hills and took off the head of a Hessian soldier, in one clean

## A haunting

Many of the soldiers, and some say the headless Hessian too, were eventually laid to rest in the Old Dutch Burial Ground in Sleepy Hollow. Yet he does not sleep. I am told he rises each night at midnight, mounts his horse, and gallops off in search of his head unfairly taken in battle. But will any head do?

## Fact or folklore?

I wonder, have the lines between fact and folklore blurred like ink bleeding across the page? Years later, Tarrytown author Washington Irving penned the classic ghost story "The Legend of Sleepy Hollow." It was so popular that the northern end of Tarrytown, where the Old Dutch Graveyard lies, was eventually renamed Sleepy Hollow in its honor.

So, is the headless horseman a tale, or true terror? I journey into Sleepy Hollow to find out.

# CONFRONTING THE HEADLESS HORSEMAN

Haunted tales are woven into the fabric of this town. From ghostbusters quietly summoned to banish spirits from more than one manor house, to the Woman in White who shrieks at the sky to ward off bad weather. And so, superstitious townsfolk line the lonely streets with blazing jack-o'-lanterns to ward off evil spirits. I hope they work.

## Watch your step

I reach the Old Dutch Graveyard, sprawled across the hillside on the edge of town, and tiptoe through its gates—careful to not wake any headless spirits. All around me the trees sway, like wiry witches worshiping the moon. A screech owl's call slices through the night. With teeth chattering, I remind myself to not lose my head.

## The witching hour has come

As my watch hands tick to midnight the wolfish wind begins to howl. It whips the mist high off the ground, swirling it through the night, to settle into the horrifying form of a black horse and its ghostly rider. My gaze travels up, up, up, and I see a uniformed body, a stiff collar, and absolutely nothing upon it. THERE IS NO HEAD!

## He rises!

All the warnings I have read echo through my mind: "he searches for a head unfairly taken!" Then the horseman's voice suddenly cuts through the night: "Yours will do!"

And as he lowers his blade to my neck . . . I run!

## Galloping through the graveyard

Hoofbeats trample the earth behind me as I frantically weave between headstones. Gasping for breath, I finally reach the graveyard's iron gates, and shut them with a SLAM.

At once both horse and rider dissolve into the night—locked in a past they cannot escape.

A relieved smile tugs at the corner of my mouth. I have investigated the last horrible haunting and can finally go home.

## Case closed.

# THIS. ENDS. NOW.

And just like that, the Ghost Hunter's words run out,
as though he simply vanished.

Or was it the curse?

Because when you try to close the book, the wolfish wind gasps and gusts, as a rage-filled roar slams the cabin shutters. Every evil thing the Ghost Hunter trapped inside the Book of Frights is now attempting to get out. His warning on the first page suddenly comes back to haunt you: "Open it at your peril."

So long as the Book of Frights is open . . . the spirits are free to escape.

Suddenly a clawed hand reaches for you through the page. There's no time to lose—you must close the book and trap them inside for good.

Unseen hands pry the book from your grasp and hurl it across the room beyond your reach. Quick as a flash, you scramble across the floor as the room begins to shake. Like a tightly coiled spring, you launch yourself toward the book, and . . .

. . . **SLAM.** You tackle it shut.

At once it's as though all the air in the room is sucked inside the Book of Frights, as one by one, each evil spirit disappears into its pages. The Headless Horseman, the Mackenzie Poltergeist, and Pan— his sharp hooves flailing.

# IT IS OVER.

# THE CURSE IS BROKEN

You can't risk someone else foolishly opening the book as you did, so you quietly slip out the back door, into the woods. You decide to bury it, so that the earth can swallow the beastly book whole.

With the hole dug, you coil a rusty bike chain around the book, snap the padlock shut, and fling it into the ground.

"Good riddance," you smile, as you hurriedly fill in the hole.

Satisfied, you slap your hands together and turn back for the cabin. As the wolfish wind howls, you decide that should anyone ever ask . . .

## . . . THERE IS NO SUCH THING AS GHOSTS!

# TALL TALES AND RIPPING YARNS

## Ancient ghosts

One of the first images of a ghost can be traced back to the ancient civilization of Babylon (modern-day Iraq). Etched into a clay tablet from 1500 BCE is the image of a ghost being led back to the Afterlife, though the image can only be seen by lamplight. The tablet leaves readers with the final, haunting line ". . . not look behind you."

## The original haunted house

In the 1st century, the Roman author Pliny the Younger wrote to a friend describing a haunted house in Athens, Greece. He said a ghost would appear nightly, clanking its chains until it drove the fearful homeowners away. Then, one night when the clanging began, a new owner followed the ghost into the courtyard, where it faded into the cobblestones. The cobbles were dug up the next day, where a skeleton was discovered in chains. With a proper burial arranged, the hauntings ceased, for the spirit was at last set free.

## That spooky time of year

Through the centuries, many cultures have found comfort in the long dark months of winter by huddling around a fire to share tales of the supernatural. The Victorians of nineteenth-century England were especially fond of ghost stories at Christmas. The most famous is Charles Dickens' A Christmas Carol from 1843, where four phantoms visit a moneylender to scare him out of his wicked ways.

## The birth of Halloween

More than 2,000 years ago in Ireland, the Celtic tribes would hold a festival on October 31 known as Samhain (pronounced sow-in), to mark the end of the fall harvest and the beginning of winter. On that night, they believed the line between the living and dead became thin, allowing spirits to cross into our world. To frighten away evil spirits, turnips were carved into jack-o'-lanterns, bonfires lit, and costumes donned as disguises. In time, Samhain became known as All Hallows' Eve—later shortened to Halloween.

Now, sleep tight ghost hunters. Perhaps next time choose your bedtime book more carefully, for some books are really, truly frightful.

## THE END

# GLOSSARY

**Acropolis**—Meaning "high city," it is a fortified part of an ancient Greek city built on a hill.

**Afterlife**—In some beliefs, the place where people go after they die.

**American Revolution**—A war that raged between 1775 and 1783, during which Americans fought Britain for independence in thirteen British colonies in North America. The colonies went on to establish the United States of America.

**Banshee**—A supernatural being from Irish folklore that is said to wail at night.

**Catacomb**—An underground cemetery.

**Celtic**—A term used to describe the Celts, a group of tribes that spread through Europe from around 1200 BCE.

**Cistern**—A man-made water tank or reservoir.

**Closes**—Narrow alleyways between tall tenement apartments.

**Convict**—A person who has been found guilty of a crime and sent to prison.

**Djinn**—According to Islamic mythology, a magical spirit that lives on earth, but is unseen by humans.

**Fen**—A low, flat wetland.

**Hessian**—A German soldier who fought with the British during the American Revolution.

**Kirkyard**—A term mostly used in Scotland for a churchyard.

**Mausoleum**—An above-ground, stone building used to house the dead.

**Menagerie**—A collection of wild, often exotic animals, for private or public viewing.

**Middle Ages**—A period in European history from around 400 to 1500 CE, between the collapse of the Roman Empire and the beginning of the Renaissance when arts, science, and culture flourished.

**Norman**—A member of the Norwegian Vikings who settled in northern France in the 900s CE, and invaded England in 1066.

**Orbs**—A ball, especially of light or energy.

**Outlaw**—A person who has broken the law and is on the run to escape punishment.

**Paranormal phenomenon**—An unnatural event or experience that cannot be explained by science.

**Penal colony**—A remote settlement where prisoners were sent to live or work, often on islands or far from their home.

**Phantom**—A ghost of a dead person who appears in the living world.

**Pharaoh**—An ancient Egyptian ruler.

**Plague**—An infectious disease spread by rats that was responsible for the death of millions of people throughout history.

**Poltergeist**—A supernatural force or noisy ghost responsible for breaking and moving things inside a house.

**Smuggler**—A person who illegally transports goods into or out of a country.

**Tenement**—A large building, especially in Scotland or the United States, where its many stories are divided into apartments.

**Treason**—A crime in which a person betrays or helps to overthrow their country or government.

**Triskaidekaphobia**—Fear of the number thirteen.

**Valley of the Kings**—A royal burial ground for the ancient rulers of Egypt, near Thebes on the west bank of the Nile.

**Witch hunts**—Events in which people are accused of witchcraft, and often killed, for having opinions others felt were dangerous or evil.

**Yeoman Warder**—A colorfully uniformed royal bodyguard who protects the Tower of London. Also known as "beefeaters," the guards have existed since Tudor times in the 1400s.